CLIMBING TREES
and MUDDY KNEES

TRACK wildlife, NAVIGATE by the stars, and DISCOVER the great outdoors

By Chris Oxlade
Illustrated by Eva Sassin

CONTENTS

TIME TO GO WILD!

Where do you go to have fun? Have you discovered the great outdoors? No? Then it's time to go wild! Go exploring, see amazing natural sights, have loads of fun, and learn how to survive outside!

Discover some of the important skills you'll need to survive in the wild, such as sorting out your survival kit, building camps, getting water, signaling for help if you need to and learning essential first aid.

Or do you want to become an intrepid adventurer? Learn how to tie knots, build a dam and a raft and send messages without using a phone.

You can amaze your friends by becoming an expert tracker. Find out how to carefully follow the marks and signs left by birds and animals.

What more do you need to have a great adventure in the wild? Get reading, and then get exploring!

WILD SAFETY

• Never go exploring in the wild without an adult.

• Ask an adult before you do any of the projects in this book. In particular, ask before going near or in water, going to the coast, exploring in bad weather or in the dark, and using a GPS.

CARING FOR THE ENVIRONMENT

Always take care of the environment when you are in the wild. That means:

• Never damage rocks, animals, or plants.

• Take special care to keep fires under control, and make sure a fire is out completely before you leave it.

SURVIVAL STUFF

THE KIT YOU NEED TO SURVIVE

You never know exactly what nature will throw at you when you head out into the wild! It's wise to have a survival kit in your backpack. You can use your kit for some of the projects later in the book.

Put together a survival kit

Here are all the bits and pieces you will need.

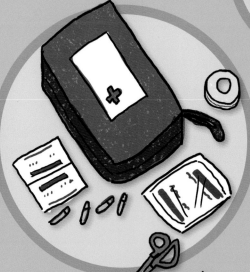

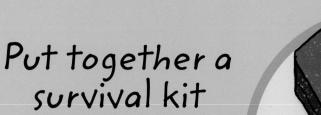

An emergency thermal blanket to keep you warm if you need to wait for help

A small metal tin or plastic box to store your survival kit

A simple first-aid kit containing a few bandages, a gauze pad, and some safety pins

A small mirror

A whistle

A few yards of paracord (a strong, nylon cord)

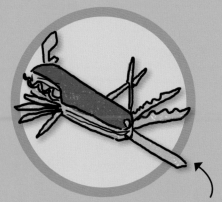

A pocketknife or multi-tool (be sure to ask an adult)

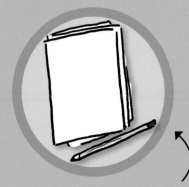

A pencil and a few small sheets of paper

A fire steel and flint for lighting a fire

KNIFE SAFETY

You'll need a knife to complete some of the projects in this book.

When using a knife, always:
- ask an adult first
- hold the knife firmly
- cut away from your body, arms and legs, never towards them
- fold away or put away your knife whenever you are not using it
- ask an adult about the law on owning and using a knife

Some waterproof matches

Emergency food, such as snack bars and nuts

A button compass

A flashlight with spare batteries

A few yards of fishing line and some small fishing hooks

FIGHTING FEAR

If you can stay calm when others are panicking, you have a better chance of survival! So try to:

- keep cool and collected

- make the right decisions at all times—for example, never cross a raging river

- prepare for the worst but hope for the best

- never give up!

TAKE COVER!

Spider tent

BUILDING A SHELTER

The weather can be a terrible foe in the wild. Wind and rain make you chilly and damp, and strong sunshine can fry you to a crisp. Luckily, it's not too tricky to craft a shelter that'll keep the elements (and some wild beasts) at bay.

Argh! Bear!

A lean-to shelter

The simplest of all ...

1. Find a tree with a branch sticking out about 3 feet (1 m) (1 m) above the ground.

2. Find a branch about 8 feet (2.5 m) (2.5 m) long. Rest one end in the V between the tree trunk and the branch to make a top beam for your shelter.

WHERE TO BUILD?

You can build your shelter pretty much anywhere, but steer clear of places like hilltops, where you could be blown away, or right next to streams or in low areas where you could be flooded out.

3. Lean plenty of branches at an angle from the ground against the beam on both sides.

4. Cover the branches in dead leaves or more leafy branches.

5. Throw more dry leaves on the ground to make your shelter more comfy.

6. Snuggle inside, feet first.

An A-frame

Can't find a tree to support your shelter? Use this handy frame instead, or use two frames to support a tent-shaped shelter.

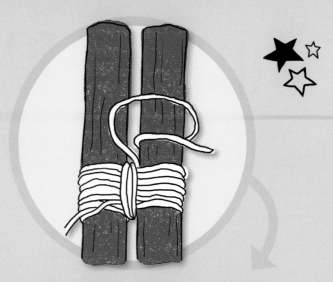

1. Tie the end of a piece of paracord to a 5-foot-long (15 m) stick, about 10 inches (25 cm) from one end, with a clove hitch as shown above.

2. Put another stick next to the first one.

3. Wrap the cord around both sticks about 10 times but not too tightly.

4. Wrap the cord tightly around the turns of rope between the two sticks twice.

5. Using the clove hitch again, tie the end of the rope around the second stick.

6. That's it! Pull the ends of the sticks apart to form your A-frame.

Always ask permission before tying up a friend!

WILD WARMTH

MAKING A FIRE

Fire is a lifesaver in the wild. It keeps you warm when it's cold, cooks food, lights up the dark, and wards off wild animals. To start a fire you need fuel, heat, and air.

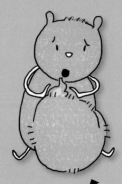

Don't catch your tail on fire!

FIRE SAFETY

You must always ask an adult before lighting a fire, whether it's in your garden or in the wild. Don't light fires when the weather has been very dry, and don't make your fire so large that it could get out of control.

Lighting a fire

1. Choose a site for your fire, well away from trees. Clear the ground and cut away turf so you can put it back later.

2. Gather tinder, kindling, and fuel (see panel).

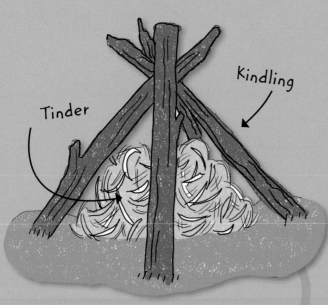

Tinder

Kindling

4. Light the tinder with a match. As the tinder begins to burn, add more tinder, then add kindling.

5. Look after your fire, feeding it with fuel all the time.

3. Lay a mat of dry, dead wood. Then arrange your kindling into a small tepee, with the tinder underneath.

6. Always make sure your fire is out and the ashes are cold before you leave. Clear the site and replace turf if you have cut it.

Making a feather stick

Use a feather stick if you can't find any small kindling to get your fire going.

1. Find a dry stick about 1/2-inch (1 cm) thick and use your knife to cut slivers of wood along the sides so the stick looks feathery.

2. Make a few feather sticks, and keep them ready in case you want to light a fire in a hurry.

BE SAFE
Read page 14 for knife safety tips before you start.

Tinder

FIRE FUEL

To get a fire going, you need:

Tinder—fluffy material that burns very easily, such as dry grass

Kindling—small twigs and other pieces of wood

Fuel—sticks and logs

It's nice to share your fire with friends.

11

Fire without matches

What happens if you drop your matches in a pond? Don't despair—you can still light a fire without them!

You won't find one of these in the wild!

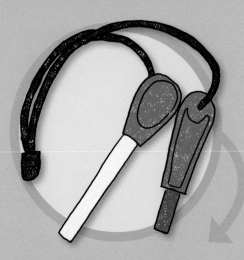

1. A flint and steel is made up of a strip of magnesium metal and a steel striker.

2. To light tinder with a flint and steel, aim the flint at the tinder, press the steel onto it, and push the steel down to make a spark. Keep trying until the tinder lights.

3. Once your tinder is smoldering, blow gently to make it burst into flames. Now you can put kindling over the tinder and get your fire going.

4. On a hot, sunny day, you can light a fire with a magnifying glass. Focus the sun's rays onto tinder until it smolders, then blow on the tinder as before.

Fire by friction

This fire-lighting method was invented thousands of years ago. It's tricky to make it work, but have a go!

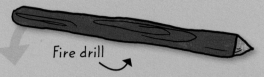
Fire drill

1. Make a fire drill from a straight stick about 20 inches (50 cm) long. Sharpen one end and make the other end rounded.

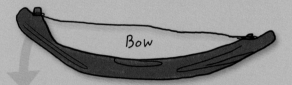
Bow

2. Make a bow from a curved branch and paracord or strong string. The string should be taut but not too tight.

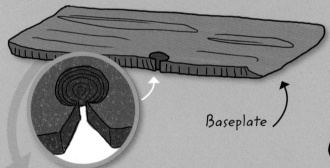
Baseplate

3. Cut a triangular notch about 3/4-inch (2 cm) deep into the side of a wooden baseplate.

4. Wrap the string of your bow once around your drill. Place the sharp end of the drill into the notch on the baseplate.

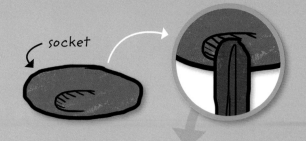
socket

5. Press down on top of the stick with a concave stone (one with a small hollow).

6. Ready to make fire? Move the bow backwards and forwards quickly. After a while, you should get black powder in the notch and a scorched hole in the wood.

7. Gradually move the bow faster and faster until the drill begins to smoke. Go faster still, and you should create a glowing ember in the pile of powder.

8. Transfer the ember to a heap of kindling and blow gently to make flames.

FOR THE CHOP

USING A KNIFE

In the wild you often need to make stuff from the bits of wood you find around you. So you need a knife and the skills to use it properly.

Pocketknife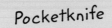

KNIFE SAFETY

Always ask an adult before using a knife, and make sure you know the local laws about carrying knives. Always keep knives folded up or sheathed when not in use.

Sheath knife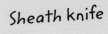

Using a pocketknife safely

1. Here's how to hold a knife safely. This forehand grip allows you to push down firmly on the knife to make a cut.

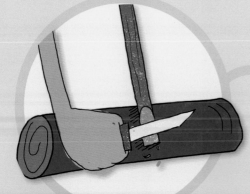

2. To make a cut in a stick, first sit down on the ground. Keep the knife and the stick in front of your knees all the time, and cut away from your body. Remember to fold up or sheath the knife afterwards.

3. To make deeper cuts, or to cut harder wood, rest the stick on a tree trunk or large log. The same rule applies—always cut away from your body.

Making a walking stick

So heavy!

1. Find a branch about 1 inch (2 cm) thick and about 8 feet (2.5 m) long. Ask an adult to saw off the ends if you can only find a longer branch.

3. Make similar cuts at the other end of the branch, this time to form a blunt end.

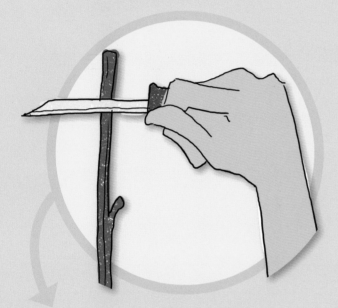

2. Cut diagonally through the branch close to one end. Make more cuts to form a sharp point. Make a few small cuts rather than one or two big ones.

4. Decorate your stick by cutting notches along the sides. To make a notch, rest your stick on a tree trunk or log, make a shallow cut at angle, then angle the blade the other way and make another cut. Remove the cut wood.

Walking sticks aren't very helpful when you're a bird!

Left! Left! Left, Right, Left!

THIRSTY WORK

FINDING WATER

You can't survive without water. So if you're in the wild in need of a drink but there isn't a river or stream close by, you need to know how to find water.

WATER SAFETY

Never drink water you've found in the wild without sterilizing it first (with special tablets or by boiling it). Never drink saltwater. And never drink your own pee.

Water from leaves

You can capture the water that is always evaporating from the leaves of plants.

Remember to remove bugs before you sterilize your water!

1. Carefully put a clear plastic bag over the end of a branch of a tree or bush. Close the neck of the bag and tie it loosely with string.

2. Wait for a few hours, then examine the bag. You should find water has collected in the bottom.

Water from grass

Collect dew from the grass in the early morning by tying towels to your legs and walking around. Then simply squeeze the water from the towels.

Water from the Sun

That's not water from the sun itself, but getting water using the sun's energy!

1. Find a sunny spot, and dig a shallow pit about 1 foot (30 cm) deep in the ground. Place a dish or other container in the center of the pit.

2. Put some fresh leaves in and cover the pit with a plastic sheet. Put stones around the edge to hold the plastic sheet in place, and put a small stone in the center of the sheet to make it sag slightly in the center.

3. Wait a few hours! Then have a look in the container. Have you got any water?

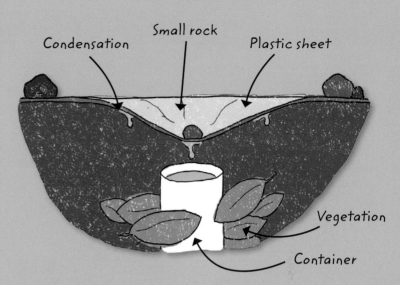

Condensation · Small rock · Plastic sheet · Vegetation · Container

Water from a frog

In a dire emergency you can get water from a frog's body. Only try this under expert supervision! And only in a dire emergency!

1. First you have to find the right sort of frog, such as the water-holding frog that lives in Western Australia! This normally means digging into the ground.

2. Simply squeeze the frog gently sideways, and be ready to catch the water in a dish or in your mouth!

Collecting rainwater

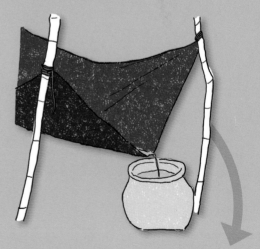

Tie the corners of a plastic sheet to the branches of a tree, with one end of the sheet lower than the other. If it rains, water will pour off the sheet. Catch it in a container.

CATCHING A FEAST

HUNTING AND FISHING

So you've built a shelter, found some water and got your fire going. All you need now is something to eat! Please don't catch any animals to eat unless it's a real survival situation.

WHAT NOT TO EAT!

We've all seen survival experts on the television eating raw fish, wriggling bugs, and nasty-looking insects. Don't try this yourself! Never eat any brightly colored animal, such as this frog, because it will probably be poisonous!

Don't eat us!
We are poisonous!

Make a bottle fish trap

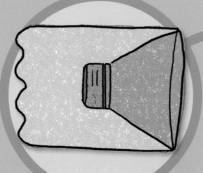

2. Reverse the top and push it into the bottle.

1. Cut the top off a plastic pop bottle.

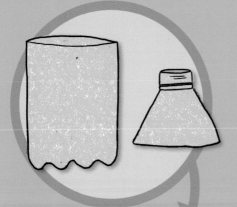

3. Put some bait, such as food scraps, into the bottle.

4. Place your trap underwater for a few hours. Look inside. Any fish?

Make a slingshot

Here's a tool you could use for hunting. Never actually fire it at a person or animal unless you're in a real survival situation.

1. Find a tree branch with a neat Y shape, such as this one. The wood should be at least 1/2 inch (30 cm) thick.

2. With a knife or saw, cut away the ends to make a Y-shaped piece of wood, about 8 inches (20 cm) long.

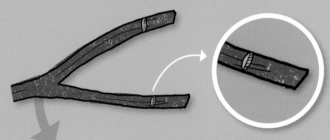

3. Cut a shallow notch about 1 inch (2 cm) from the end of each arm.

This might be a bit more than he bargained for!

4. Prepare a piece of nylon webbing or a leather strip, about 5 inches (12 cm) long. Cut a hole about 1 inch (2 cm) from each end.

5. Now you need a length of thick elastic or rubber tubing, about 24 inches (60 cm) long. Thread this through the holes in the webbing.

6. Tie the ends of the elastic around the top of the arms of the Y shape, in line with the notches.

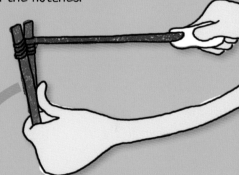

7. To fire your slingshot, put a small stone in the center of the webbing, grip the stone through the webbing from behind, pull back the webbing, take aim... and fire!

Making a fishing rod

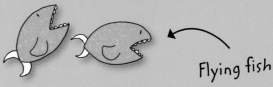

Flying fish

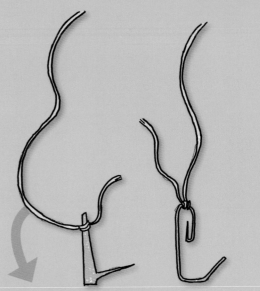

1. Look for a bendy stick at least 6.5 feet (2 m) long. A thin, freshly cut bamboo pole is perfect. Cut a small notch close to the thinner end.

2. Tie a length of string about 6.5 feet (2 m) long to the thin end of the stick where you cut the notch.

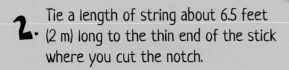

5. If you don't have a fishing hook or line, don't despair! You can make hooks from paper clips and even the thorns from prickly plants, such as hawthorn.

6. You can also try fishing with any sort of cord, such as string, cotton, wool, and even your shoe laces.

3. Add a piece of fishing line about 6.5 feet (2 m) long to the end of the string. To join the string and line, double over the end of the line and tie a loop, then tie the string to the loop.

4. Now tie a fishing hook to the line with a half blood knot, as shown.

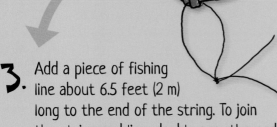

1

2

3

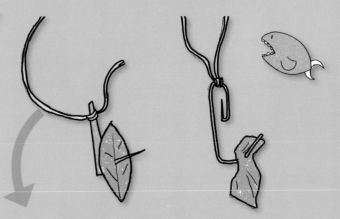

7. For bait you can use food scraps or objects that look like a small fish underwater.

8. Drop your hook and bait into the water. Now wait patiently. If your line wiggles, pull up sharply on the fishing rod to hook the fish.

20

IF YOU CATCH A FISH...

Don't panic! Wet your hands and hold the fish firmly but not tightly. Carefully remove the hook from the fish's mouth, then return the fish to the water. Always release fish that you don't need for survival.

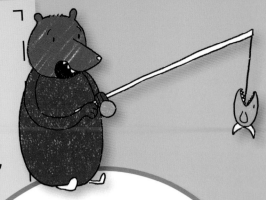

Spit fishing

1. Stand in the water, and spit into the water in front of you.

2. Wait with your t-shirt ready to scoop up fish attracted to the spit. Simple!

FISHING, SAFETY AND THE LAW

Never go fishing without an adult, and never fish where there is a chance of falling into deep, cold, or fast-flowing water. Also, be careful of sharp hooks. You should use barbless hooks, which are easier to get out of fish and fingers than barbed ones. Make sure you know the laws about fishing—in many places you need a licence to fish.

Fishing by hand

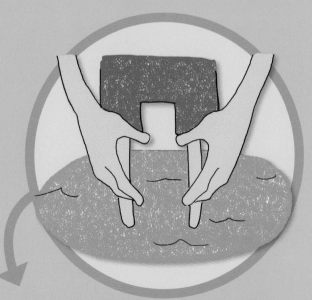

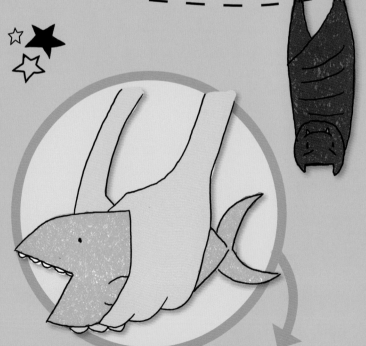

1. Stand very still in shallow water, up to 1 foot (30 cm) deep, with your hands cupped.

2. Wait for a fish to come close, then very, very slowly, move your hands around it, and grab it!

WILD FARE

FORAGING FOR FOOD

Plants are on the menu in the wild, as are fish and other animals. And catching plants is much easier than catching animals! Check out some of the yummy berries, nuts, and leaves you can eat.

Collecting berries and nuts

Nuts and berries are a good source of energy.

1. Blackberries, blueberries, and cranberries are all edible. You can eat them raw or stew them in a pot over your campfire.

2. Search for nuts, such as hazelnuts and sweet chestnuts, which you can eat raw. Collect acorns, too, but boil them a few times in water to stop them from tasting bitter.

Blueberries

Blackberries

Cranberries

Hazelnuts

Acorns

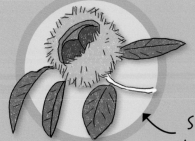

Sweet chestnuts

Sssssss-so tasty!

Collecting leaves

Eating leaves might not seem ideal, but many herbs are leaves and so are salad ingredients. You can find similar leaves to eat in the wild.

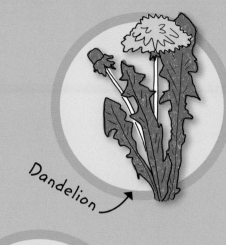
Dandelion

1. Search for dandelion, sorrel, and stinging nettle leaves. You can also eat watercress if you find it near rivers.

Sorrel

Stinging nettle

2. You can make delicious tea from stinging nettles. Pick the leaves of young plants, wearing gloves to avoid being stung. Wash the leaves with fresh water.

3. Put the leaves in a pan of boiling water and boil them for a few minutes, until the water looks slightly green. Allow the water to cool a little before drinking. Don't worry, the nettles can't sting any more!

I shouldn't have eaten ALL the blackberries!

Don't eat me! I am purple, but I am not a blackberry!

23

FOOD ON FIRE

COOKING OVER A CAMPFIRE

If you've found some food to eat in the wild, you can make a fire (see page 10) and cook the food over it. To practice cooking over a fire, try these projects with food from home.

Making a pot support

Here's how to suspend a kettle over a fire for heating and purifying water in a pot.

1. Find a stick or branch with a fork in it. Shorten the ends to make a stick with a forked end, about 20 inches (50 cm) long. Sharpen the single end.

2. Push the stick into the ground close to your fire but not so close that it will burn.

3. Find a stick about 5 feet (1.5 m) long. Cut off the side branches, then cut a deep notch about 1 inch (2 cm) from the thin end of the stick.

4. Place the long stick in the support, so that one end rests on the ground and the other end is over the fire, high enough so that it doesn't burn. Use a log or large stone to hold the stick steady.

Now you can make some nettle tea (see page 23)!

5. Hang your kettle in the notch, being careful of the fire.

24

Cooking in foil

Use this method for cooking potatoes and other vegetables in your fire.

1. Wrap your potatoes, parsnips, or bits of rutabaga in foil and drop them in the center of the fire. Keep your hands away from the flames.

2. Give the vegetables half an hour to cook. Use a stick to roll them out of the fire, then ask an adult to unwrap them.

Making a skewer

Any food that you can put on a skewer can be cooked over your fire. That includes marshmallows, sausages, and vegetables.

1. Make a support for the pot as you did before.

2. Find thin, green sticks and shave off the bark to make skewers.

Even when cooked, worms will probably be icky!

3. Attach a skewer to a longer stick by wrapping string around both. Push your food onto the skewer and rest the stick in the support so that the food is over the fire.

I'm a survival chef!

SOS!

Don't light your fire until you are ready!

CALLING FOR HELP

If you're trapped in the wild, you need to know how to call for help. There probably won't be a mobile phone signal where you are—or maybe you dropped your phone in a river! Never call for help unless there is a real emergency.

Fire signals

Bright flames will attract rescuers at night, and smoke will attract rescuers in the day. Light your rescue fire in a clearing on a hilltop.

1. First, gather up all the fuel you need for a fire, and build a fire so that it is ready to light (see page 10).

2. Keep a look out. Only light your fire when help is in sight. In the day, make smoke by putting branches with green leaves over the fire.

3. Remember to put the fire out after you have been rescued.

Make a heliograph

You can use a mirror—which you should have in your survival kit—to signal, using light from the Sun. This is called a heliograph.

1. Hold the heliograph so that it bounces sunlight towards the ground (you can also use a metal tin or pair of glasses to reflect from the Sun). Practice moving the spot by tilting the heliograph left or right and up or down.

2. To send an SOS, signal an aircraft with three short flashes, three long flashes, and three short flashes again.

GROUND-TO AIR-SIGNALS

These internationally agreed signals will work anywhere in the world!

I = Serious injury

F = Need food and water

A = Yes

N = No

X = Unable to move

→ = Moving this way

LL = All is well

Ground signals

Make shapes on the ground that can be seen from the air.

1. Find a large open space that can be seen from the air.

2. Make a signal as large as possible using branches, by clearing leaves, or leaving footprints in snow.

Serious injury

Need food and water

Yes

No

Unable to move

Moving this way

All is well

PACK YOUR KIT

ADVENTURER'S EQUIPMENT

Every successful adventure starts with a little planning. And that includes gathering together all the adventure kit you might need. To start with, you'll need to take your survival kit (see pages 6 and 7. You'll also need suitable clothing and some sturdy shoes or boots. The clothes you should take will depend on the weather. So if it's roasting hot, you'll need cool clothes and a hat, and if it's raining or freezing cold, take a waterproof coat, a hat, and gloves.

An adventurer's pack

Here's a list of stuff to put in your backpack:

A pair of gloves

A hat

A bivvy bag, or a sleeping bag with weatherproofing

A waterproof tarp (about 6.5 feet [2 m] square)

Make sure you have a comfortable backpack with plenty of pockets

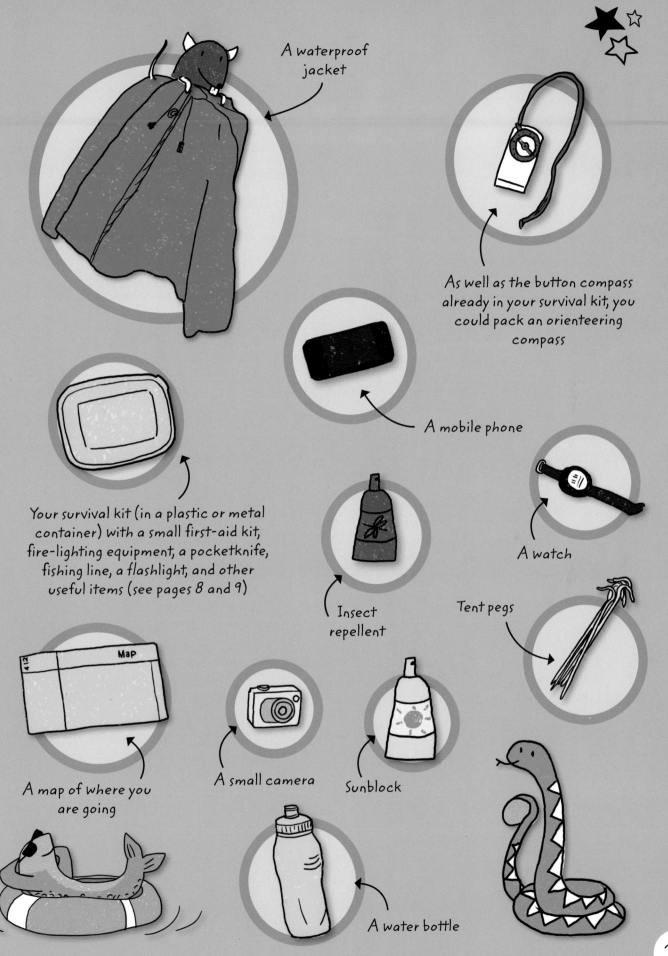

A waterproof
jacket

As well as the button compass
already in your survival kit, you
could pack an orienteering
compass

A mobile phone

A watch

Your survival kit (in a plastic or metal
container) with a small first-aid kit,
fire-lighting equipment, a pocketknife,
fishing line, a flashlight, and other
useful items (see pages 8 and 9)

Insect
repellent

Tent pegs

Map

A map of where you
are going

A small camera

Sunblock

A water bottle

29

ROPE TRICKS

ADVENTURER'S KNOTS

It would be foolish to head out into the wild without knowing a few basic knots. Adventurers need knots for building shelters, making tools, and building rafts. So find a scrap of rope and start practicing.

A clove hitch

This is a knot for attaching a rope to a branch or pole, and it is easy to undo. It's also handy when lashing branches together (see page 9). There are two ways to tie it:

Method 1: For a branch

1. Pass the end of a rope over and around the branch, then over itself.

2. Pass the end around the branch again.

3. Thread the end under the second loop.

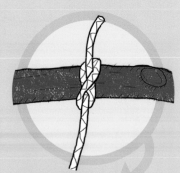

4. Pull tight.

Method 2: For a post

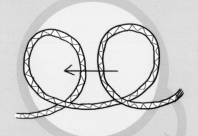

1. Form two loops near the end of the rope.

2. Place one loop over the other loop.

3. Drop the loops over a post and pull tight.

A bowline

Use this knot for attaching a rope to a thick tree or a fellow adventurer's waist.

1. Pass the rope around the tree, then make a loop in the main rope.

2. Thread the end through the loop and around the main rope.

3. Thread the end back through the loop and pull tight.

A round turn and two half hitches

Use this strong knot for attaching a rope to a branch or post. It's also good for tying guy lines to trees, or a boat to the shore.

1. Wrap the end of the rope around the branch twice. (That's the round turn.)

2. Pass the end under the main rope and back over itself.

3. Pull the rope tight. That's one half hitch.

4. Repeat steps 2 and 3. That's two half hitches.

Haha! Tied you up!

A figure-eight knot

This easy knot is useful for stopping a rope sliding through a hole.

1. Fold the end of the rope behind the main rope to make an eye. Then bring the end in front of the rope again.

2. Now thread the end back through the eye.

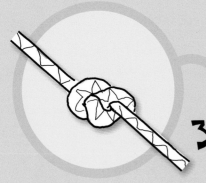

3. Pull tight.

A reef knot

Use this knot to tie together two pieces of rope that are the same thickness.

1. Pass the end of the right-hand rope over the left-hand rope, behind it, then over it again.

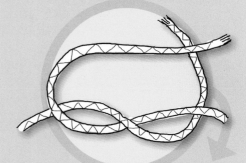

2. Pass the end of the right-hand rope over the end of the left-hand rope.

3. Thread the left-hand rope under the right-hand rope, and pull tight.

Doh!

A lashing

This knot is handy for tying two branches together at right angles to each other.

1. Place one branch over the other. Tie the end of the rope to the bottom branch with a clove hitch (see page 30).

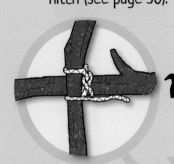

2. Pass the rope over the top branch, under the bottom branch, and back over the top branch.

3. Pass the rope back under the bottom branch, repeat step 2, then wrap the rope around the top branch.

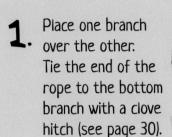

4. Wind the rope twice around the ropes between the two branches.

5. Tie a clove hitch around the top branch to finish the knot.

A sheet bend

Use this knot for tying a thick rope to a thin rope.

1. Bend over the end of the thick rope, then pass the thin rope through the bend.

2. Pass the thin rope around the back of the thick rope.

3. Thread the thin rope under itself, and pull tight.

TAKE COVER!

MAKING A SHELTER

A tarp is a waterproof sheet. Tent groundsheets, plastic sheets, and builders' tarpaulins are all tarps. They are very versatile in the wild, especially for making shelters and rafts (see page 37).

A tarp tent

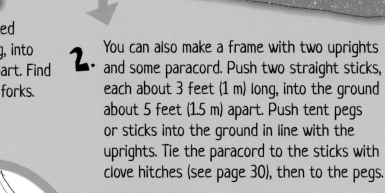

1. Make a frame by pushing two forked sticks, each about 3 feet (1 m) long, into the ground about 5 feet (1.5 m) apart. Find a stick long enough to rest in the forks.

2. You can also make a frame with two uprights and some paracord. Push two straight sticks, each about 3 feet (1 m) long, into the ground about 5 feet (1.5 m) apart. Push tent pegs or sticks into the ground in line with the uprights. Tie the paracord to the sticks with clove hitches (see page 30), then to the pegs.

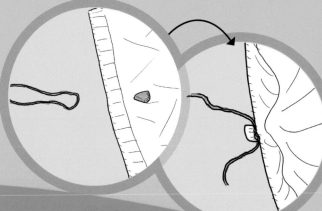

4. Tie the pieces of paracord to tent pegs in the ground and tighten them.

3. Put your tarp over the frame. If it has eyes in the corners, tie short pieces of paracord to them. If there are no eyes, fold a pebble into each corner of the tarp and hold it in place with a piece of paracord.

A tarp tunnel shelter

A tunnel shelter keeps out wind and rain better than a simple tarp shelter, but there's not as much space inside.

1. First make an A-frame by lashing together two sticks about 3 feet (1 m) long (see page 39).

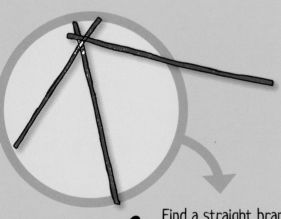

2. Find a straight branch about 6.5 feet (2 m) long and tie one end into the A-frame with a lashing.

3. Put your tarp over the frame. Hold the edges down with rocks or logs.

Watch out for bears!

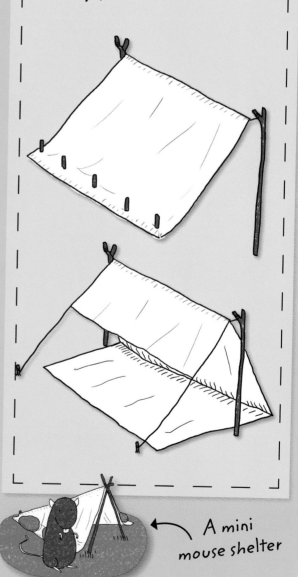

MORE SHELTER DESIGNS

Here are a couple more designs for tarp shelters. The first works with a small tarp, and the second gives you a dry place to lie down.

A mini mouse shelter

FLOATING FUN

MAKING RAFTS

Imagine you are on an adventure and there's a deep river or a lake in your way. The only thing to do is to build yourself a raft. Try one of these simple designs:

RAFT SAFETY

Only use these rafts with adult supervision. Always wear a buoyancy aid in or on water. Never go rafting on a fast-flowing river or in very cold water.

Bottle raft

1. Collect up lots of plastic bottles! You'll need about 30 2-liter bottles for this raft. Start arranging the bottles on a piece of thin board about 3 feet (1 m) square.

2. Once the board is covered with bottles, attach them to the board with strong tape, such as duck tape, or with cord. Secure the tape or cord right around the bottles and the board.

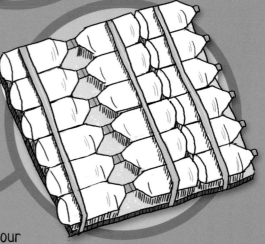

3. Grab a stick, sit on your raft and paddle away!

Watch out for piranha!

36

Donut Raft

1. Spread out a tarp about 6.5 feet (2 m) square—one designed to make a shelter works well. Gather up bushy branches and arrange them into a donut shape on the tarp. Tie the branches together loosely with string or cord.

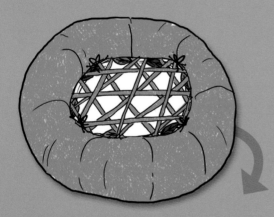

2. Fold the edges of the tarp into the center of the donut. Tuck the edges under the branches, or tie the edges together.

3. There should be a hole in the center for you to sit in, with your legs dangling over the side. Make sure you don't puncture the tarp! Paddle with a stick.

Log raft

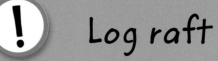

1. Find six or more logs at least 4 inches across and at least 5 feet long. **These will be heavy, so ask an adult to help you collect them.**

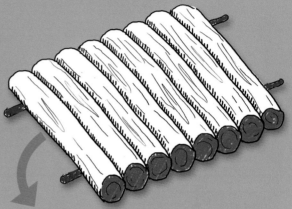

2. Place two strong sticks on the ground, about 3 feet (1 m) apart. Lay your logs side by side on top of the sticks. Now lay two more sticks on top of the logs above the first two sticks.

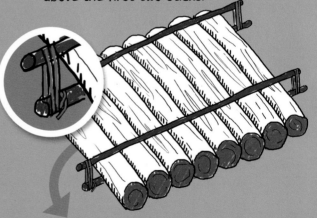

3. Tie the ends of the sticks together tightly with cord. Start with a clove hitch (see page 30) around one stick, then wind the cord around the sticks a few times, and tie the loose end of the cord with another clove hitch.

SINK OR SWIM

WATERY HAZARDS

Out in the wild, there probably won't be a bridge for crossing a shallow stream or river, so you need the skills to get across safely. Take care—it's not always easy to tell how deep the water is—and if in doubt, don't cross.

RIVER SAFETY

Practice these skills crossing only small, shallow (that means ankle-deep) streams and only under adult supervision. Never try to cross any stream or river that's more than knee-deep, fast-flowing, or very wide. Flowing water is very powerful, and there is a high risk of being swept off your feet.

Never cross a stream or river where there are hazards such as rapids, waterfalls, or log jams, or on bends where the water flows fast.

How to wade across a stream

1. In an emergency, if you have to cross a stream on your own, use a walking stick or pole to help you to balance. Face upstream, and shuffle sideways. Move one foot at a time, making sure you get a good foothold.

Move this way

Water Flow

2. This is one way to cross a stream in a group. Form a ring, so that two people can support you as you move your feet. Only one person moves at a time.

Move this way

Water Flow

3. A group can also cross in a line, one behind the other, all facing upstream. The front person uses a stick for balance, and the others support him or her. Everybody moves slowly sideways, keeping in line.

Water Flow

Move this way

How to escape from quicksand

If you are on a riverbank or a beach, you might come across quicksand. Follow these tips to escape. The same tricks work if you fall in a bog.

1. The first trick is to stay calm! Don't wriggle around! Keep still and you won't sink. Throw off your backpack to reduce your weight.

2. If you are only up to your knees, sit down. If you are in deeper, lean back, so that your weight is spread across the sand.

3. Now pull your legs out. Do this with very small movements, and very slowly! Then crawl to safety, keeping flat to spread out your weight.

WATER WALLS

BUILDING DAMS

You can build a dam across a stream to make a small pond for cooling down with a paddle or for catching fish. Make sure you have permission to build a dam, and always dismantle your dam before you leave.

A stone dam

1. A stone dam needs to be wide at the base and narrow at the top, with sloping sides. Start by placing large rocks side by side, building a base 15 to 20 inches wide.

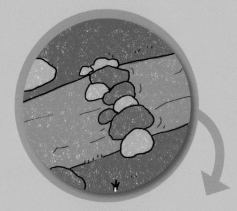

2. Add more rocks on top of the base, gradually building a wall that slopes front and back.

4. Push gravel or sand onto the back wall so that the water will wash it into the gaps. Wait for the water to build up behind your dam.

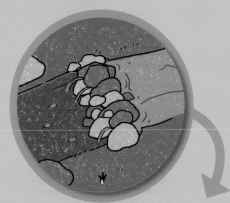

3. Water will leak through the gaps between the stones, so now find small stones to block the holes as well as you can. The water will help to push them into place.

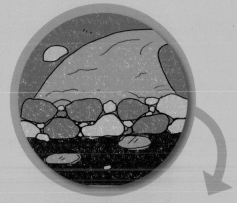

5. Remember to knock down your dam before you go home.

A stick dam

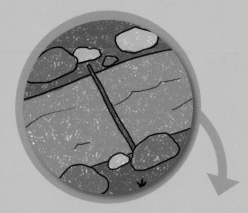

1. Find a branch long enough to stretch from one bank of the stream to the other. Stamp the ends down to help keep them in place.

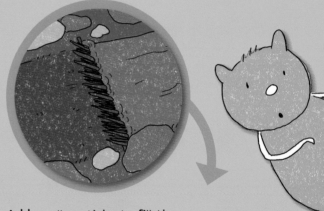

CHOOSING A DAM SITE
Only build a dam in a small, shallow stream—never in fast-flowing or deep water. A stream 3 to 7 feet across with a flat bed and high banks, is the easiest place to build one.

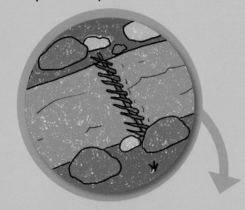

2. Find sticks to fit between the log and the stream bed. Angle them so their ends are further upstream then the log. Put the sticks as close together as you can.

Argh! Heavy!

3. Add smaller sticks to fill the gaps between the larger sticks.

4. Finally, cover the sticks with leaves to block up any remaining gaps.

5. Wait for the water to build up behind your dam. Knock down your dam before you go home.

WILD SIGNS

SENDING MESSAGES

Out in the wild, remember your mobile phone probably won't get a signal, or its battery could go dead. No problem! There are other ways to send messages to your companions.

Signaling the way

You can leave signs on the ground to record your route or to show your companions the way you have gone.

Arrow made with rocks

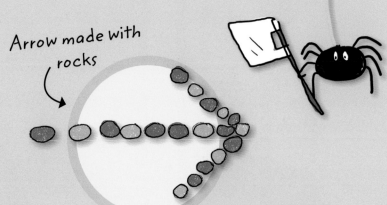

Pointing stick supported by forked stick

Arrow made with sticks

Arrow made with flour

Hmmm, which way?

Spots of flour

Crossed sticks mean "not this way"

Morse code messages

Morse code is handy for sending messages to a companion who can't see you (so you use blasts of a whistle) or can't hear you (so you use flashes of a flashlight).

1. Look at this Morse code sheet (it could be a useful addition to your backpack). Try a simple emergency message. This is made up of the Morse code for the letters SOS: three short blasts or flashes; a small gap, then three long blasts or flashes; a small gap, then three more short blasts or flashes.

2. You can send any message you like using Morse code, as long as you and your companions know the code.

A •—	J •———	S •••
B —•••	K —•—	T —
C —•—•	L •—••	U ••—
D —••	M ——	V •••—
E •	N —•	W •——
F ••—•	O ———	X —••—
G —••	P •——•	Y —•——
H ••••	Q ——•—	Z ——••
I ••	R •—•	

0 —————	4 ••••—	8 ———••
1 •————	5 •••••	9 ————•
2 ••———	6 —••••	
3 •••——	7 ——•••	

Semaphore messages

Here's an alternative to Morse code if you are careless enough to lose your whistle and your flashlight!

1. You'll need two flags. You can make a flag by attaching a plastic bag to the end of a stick. Or use a leafy branch instead.

2. Study the semaphore code sheet here, then try sending some messages. Keep the messages short or your arms will soon get tired!

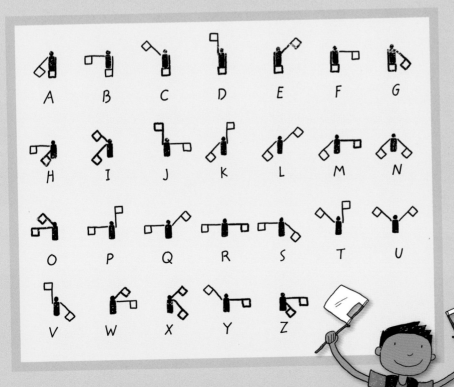

SLINGS AND SPLINTS

FIRST AID FOR ADVENTURERS

The odd bump or scrape is all part of being an adventurer. That's why you should always carry a first-aid kit. In an emergency you might need to treat more serious injuries, such as broken bones or deep cuts. Here are some skills to practice on your uninjured friends.

FIRST-AID SAFETY

First aid is a great skill to have. It's best to learn from the experts by taking a first-aid course. If an accident does happen, get adult help as fast as you can. Never try out any first aid unless you know exactly what you are doing. You could unintentionally make things worse.

Make a sling

A sling supports a broken arm or injured shoulder.

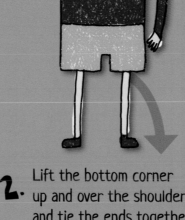

1. Open out a large triangular bandage and place it under the person's injured arm, with one end over the other shoulder.

2. Lift the bottom corner up and over the shoulder and tie the ends together behind the neck.

3. Fold the edge around the elbow and fasten it with a safety pin.

Make a splint

Here's how to make an emergency splint for a broken leg.

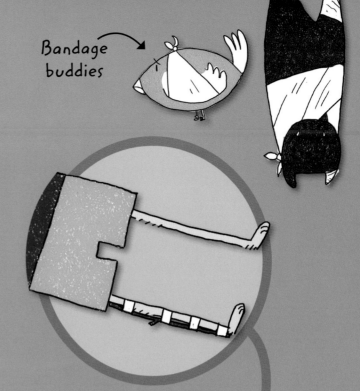

Bandage buddies

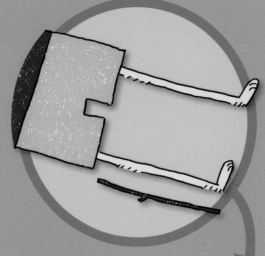

1. Do not move the injured limb, as this may make it worse. Search for a sturdy stick the same length as the injured person's leg. Place it alongside the leg.

2. Very gently and not too tightly, tie bandages around the leg and the splint, above and below the injury. This will keep the leg still until help arrives.

Duck-tape stitches

All purpose duct tape has many uses in the wild, including first aid. You can use it as an alternative to bandages for making slings and tying splints, or use it to stitch a big cut.

Wound with duck tape.

1. Wash the wound with plenty of clean water, then carefully dab dry the skin around the wound.

I've got a poorly hoof.

2. Cut or tear thin strips of duck tape about 4 inches (10 cm) long. Apply them across the wound, pressing the wound gently together as you do.

45

Charcoal medicine

Charcoal (not ashes) from the burned sticks in a cold campfire can help to settle an upset stomach and can also help to counteract poison.

1. Make sure the fire is cold. Take a burned stick and scrape off the black charcoal with another stick, into a container or onto a piece of bark.

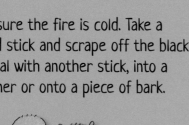

2. Eat the charcoal with plenty of water, but don't eat too much—a spoonful is enough. Did you know that charcoal can also be used to filter water to make it clean?

Muddy sunblock

You should always carry some sunblock in your backpack to prevent painful sunburn, but if you run out, there is an alternative — mud! It's a trick that some animals use.

Find a source of good, thick mud. Clay is best, and you can add water if you need to. Muddy soil doesn't work so well.

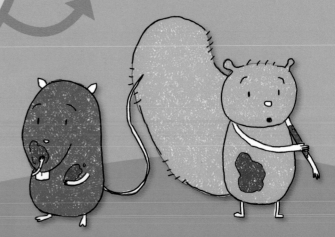

Maggot therapy

We know it sounds disgusting. But in the wild, maggots will clean an infected wound by eating away damaged flesh. Obviously, we're not suggesting you try this on a grazed knee. Keep it in reserve only for a deep and dirty wound and with adult supervision!

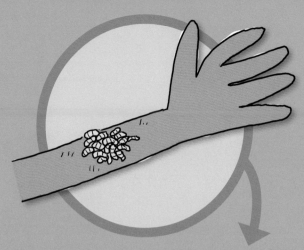

1. Leave the wound open to the air for a day, so that flies can lay eggs in it. Urgh!

2. Cover the wound. Check it each day, and you should find maggots. Even more urgh!

3. When the wound looks clean (without any pus or dirt), wash away the maggots with fresh water and bandage it up with a clean dressing.

Make an emergency stretcher

Here's how to make a stretcher to carry an injured companion to safety.

1. Find two sturdy branches, each about 6.5 feet (2 m) long. These should be stiff but not too heavy.

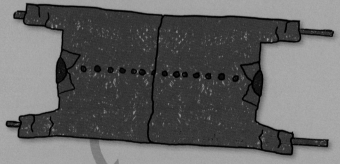

Don't always trust bears to carry your stretcher.

2. Button up two coats and push the logs through the sleeves to make a bed.

I'll lead the way!

FOLLOW THE TRACKS

ANIMAL TRACKING SKILLS

To watch animals in the wild, you first have to find them—and that means recognizing their tracks. Tracking skills will help you to follow animals by looking for footprints, paw prints, and hoof prints, and other signs left by animals.

Looking for tracks

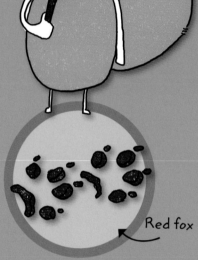

Red fox

A deer track in mud

1. The best places to search for animal tracks are muddy paths, the muddy banks of rivers, and beaches. Tracks will be clearer when the ground is damp, and early in the morning or in the evening, when the Sun is low in the sky. Walk slowly, looking carefully at the ground.

2. Try to match the tracks you find to the diagrams on this page. See if you can learn some common animal prints.

Rabbit

Cat

Grey squirrel

Deer

Dog

Black bear

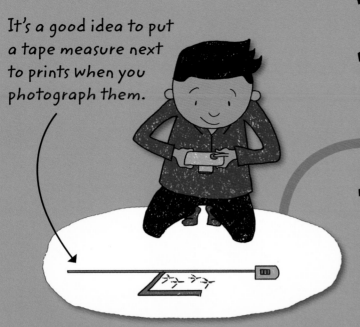

It's a good idea to put a tape measure next to prints when you photograph them.

3. In winter, tracks are easy to see in fresh snow.

4. Try taking photographs of the tracks you find. Use the close-up setting on your camera, and photograph from low down and at an angle, to make them more visible. Take photographs of lines of prints as well as single prints.

5. If you find a trail of prints, see how far you can follow them — they might lead you to an animal's home.

Detective rat

Studying bird tracks

Sandy beaches and muddy riverbanks are good places to find bird tracks. Beware of sinking in soft mud on riverbanks, though.

Chicken

Pigeon

Blackbird

Duck

Eagle

Crow

Sparrow

At the beach, look for tracks after the tide goes out; at the riverbank, look after the river level has fallen. Try to match any bird tracks you find to these diagrams.

Making molds

You can make copies of animal tracks in three dimensions. You'll need some plaster of Paris from a mold

1. Put a cardboard ring (such as the inside from a roll of sticky tape) around the print.

2. Mix a small amount of plaster of Paris, following the instructions on the packet. Carefully pour the plaster of Paris into the ring.

3. Allow the plaster of Paris to dry for about fifteen minutes, then carefully dig up the ring, taking a layer of soil with the plaster.

4. Take the ring home and leave it for a few hours to go hard. Then remove the ring and clean the dirt off the plaster.

5. Label your mold to show when and where you found the print, and what animal you think might have made the track.

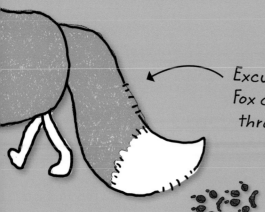

Excuse me! Fox coming through!

More signs for tracking

Animals leave other clues besides their footprints.

As you are searching for tracks, keep an eye out for nibbled bits of food and pieces of fur.

A pine cone eaten by a squirrel

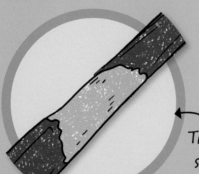

Tree bark stripped by a deer

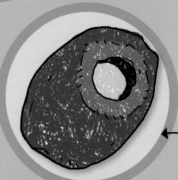

A hazel nut opened by a mouse

Poo clues

You can also identify animals by the droppings (poo) they leave.

Look out for droppings on the ground, and try to match them to the references here. Don't touch the droppings!

Deer droppings

Fox droppings

Rabbit droppings

Angry squirrel with poo on his foot!

FOLLOW THE LEADER

MAKING AND FOLLOWING TRAILS

You can have fun laying trails in the wild for your friends to follow and playing games where you creep up on your friends. These activities will be good practice for your tracking skills.

Laying a trail

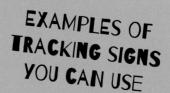

1. Organize yourself and your companions into two teams—runners and trackers. The runners set off first, laying a trail as they go. Each time they reach a junction or change direction, they leave a sign to show which way they have gone. You can do this with sticks, stones, leaves or flour.

2. The trackers wait a couple of minutes and then try to follow the signs. Can they catch the runners?

EXAMPLES OF TRACKING SIGNS YOU CAN USE

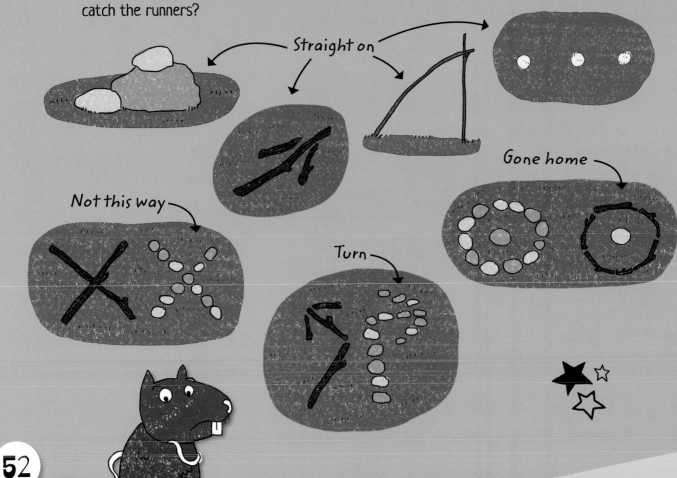

Straight on

Not this way

Turn

Gone home

Hunter and prey game

In this game, you (the hunter) try to creep up on a friend (the prey). Your friend has a water pistol and will soak you if he or she hears you. The game will help you to practice moving quietly in the wild and—if you are the one with the water pistol—to listen really carefully.

1. Choose a person to be the prey. He or she must stand in one place with a filled water pistol and wearing a blindfold. The hunters must move about 160 feet (50 m) away. When everyone is ready, the hunters must try to creep silently up to the prey and touch him or her before being heard.

2. If the prey hears a noise, he or she can fire the water pistol, aiming at where the noise came from, to try and soak the hunter.

Oops! These two have the game all wrong!

HIDE IN THE WILD

MAKING CAMOUFLAGE

When you are tracking small animals or watching birds, it's best not to let them spot you, otherwise they will get nervous and run or fly away. By wearing camouflage, you can easily blend in with the undergrowth. Or use camouflage to hide from your friends!

Camouflage face paint

2. Apply the paints to your face, in front of a mirror if possible. Use patches of color to break up the shape of your face.

3. In an emergency, you can use mud or charcoal scraped from burned sticks for face camouflage.

1. You can use face paints for this. Choose colors to match the forest and outdoors such as greens and browns, or make your own face paint by mixing skin lotion, cornstarch, and food coloring. Start with some lotion, mix the coloring in slowly, and then add cornstarch to thicken it.

A camouflage shirt

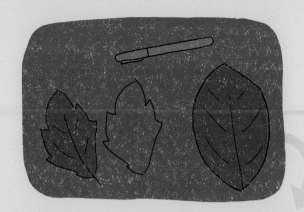

1. Visit a wooded area and collect a few large leaves. These can have just fallen to the ground or can be picked from trees.

2. Place some scraps of green cloth and brown cloth on a table. Lay your leaves on the cloth and draw around them with a marker pen. Draw about 30 leaf shapes altogether. Cut out the leaves.

3. Glue your cut-out leaves to a dark brown or dark green t-shirt with fabric glue, overlapping them to cover most of the shirt.

A camouflage hat

1. Find a dark-colored baseball cap or woolly hat. Collect up some twigs and small leafy branches, and attach these to the hat with sticky tape or safety pins.

Camouflage skunk!

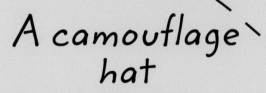

SPOT THE FLYERS

BIRD AND BAT WATCHING

By building a bird hide and a bird box you can get close to birds in the wild. This allows you to study them and perhaps spot some you have never seen before.

Oh, if only I could find a home!

Making a bird hide

Set up this bird hide in woodland or on the shore of a lake, where there are plenty of birds.

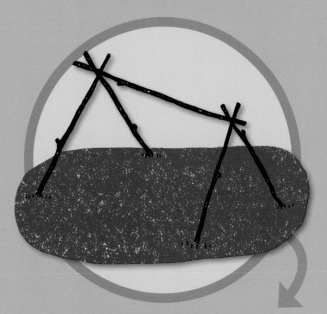

2. Lean branches against the crossbar to make a screen. Leave a space in the center of the screen to look through (you could attach some shorter branches up to a window frame). Sit behind the screen and watch quietly for birds. Use binoculars to view them more clearly.

1. Make two A-frames about 3 feet (1 m) high by lashing together two pairs of sticks about 5 feet (1.5 m) long (see page 35). Lay a crossbar between them and tie the crossbar in place.

Terwit - terwoo!

Making a nesting box

A nesting box should attract small birds looking for a place to nest.

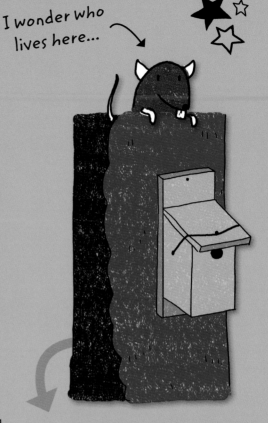

I wonder who lives here...

8 in (20 cm)	16 in (40 cm)	10 in (25 cm)	8 in (20 cm)		10 in (25 cm)
Front	Back	Side	Side	Base	Lid

6 in (15 cm)

1 inch (2 cm) hole   8 in (20 cm)   10 in (25 cm)   5 in (12 cm)

1. Cut shapes from a plank of wood, 6 inches (15 cm) wide and about a half inch (1.5 cm) thick, as shown in the diagram.

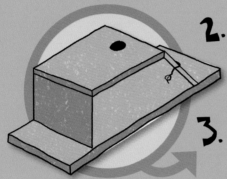

2. Glue the parts together, but leave the lid off for now.

3. Glue a small block of wood inside the lid to stop it sliding off. Also put a small screw in each side of the box and the lid, and tie a string to the screws to keep the lid on.

4. Ask an adult to help you attach your box to a tree, at least 6.5 feet (2 m) above the ground.

Looking for bats

Look for bats at dusk when they emerge from their nests to hunt insects. Take an adult with you. Good areas to look are in woodlands and along rivers.

1. Stand still, look up towards the sky and listen. Watch for small black shapes flying low and listen for high-pitched squeaks.

TWO COMMON BATS THAT YOU MIGHT SEE

Pipistrelle (UK)

Little brown bat (USA)

Hi guys!

DOWN BY THE WATER

EXPLORING PONDS AND RIVERS

You can find all sorts of creatures by exploring your local pond or stream. They live on the bottom of a pond or riverbed, in the water, and on the surface. All you need is a simple net to find them.

SAFETY NEAR WATER

Always take an adult with you when exploring near water. Be careful not to slip into the water on pond edges and riverbanks.

Pond dipping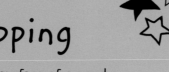

1. Start by looking above the surface of a pond or river for dragonflies, mosquitoes and other flying insects. Then search the surface itself for bugs such as whirligig beetles and pond skaters.

2. Now dip a net into the water, move it slowly through the water and lift it out. Examine the net for creatures. Try dipping at different depths, and through the mud at the bottom of the water.

COMMON ANIMALS ABOVE AND ON THE WATER

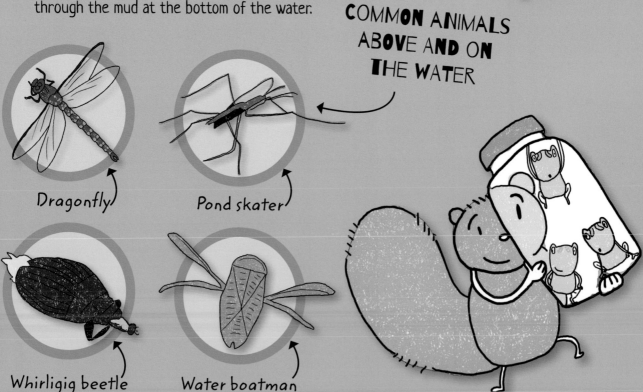

Dragonfly

Pond skater

Whirligig beetle

Water boatman

58

3. Put your captured animals into a clean jam jar or a plastic pot with some pond water inside, and examine them with a magnifying glass. Release them before going home.

Pond snail

Freshwater shrimp

Mayfly nymph

Sssso many pond animals to sssspot!

Stickleback

Newt

Looking after tadpoles

Try watching frogs' eggs grow into tadpoles.

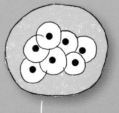

2. When the tadpoles begin to hatch, add a little fish food to the water.

3. After a few weeks, your tadpoles will start growing legs. This is the time to release them back into the pond.

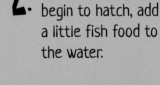

1. Collect frogspawn in the spring by dipping a jar into a pond. Only take a small amount. At home, put the frogspawn into a plastic tub with some water, and add a few stones in the bottom of the tub.

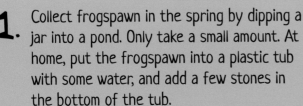

BUG BUSINESS

HUNTING AND CATCHING CREEPY CRAWLIES

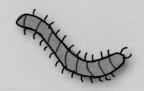

The wild is full of bugs. Millions of them! They might not be as easy to see as larger animals and birds, but you can find them if you know where to look. Then you can catch and release them.

Bug dinner

Put out tasty treats to attract some bugs to watch.

1. Make a sticky mixture of old mashed banana and sugar, smear a little on a stick, and leave the stick outdoors, under a bush or stone. Return the next day to see what creatures have been attracted. You can also look at night with a flashlight.

2. If you want to study a bug more closely, carefully lock it into a container with air holes where you can look at it with a magnifying glass.

COMMON BUGS THAT YOU MIGHT SEE

Did you see any of these common garden bugs?

Garden snail

Slug

Woodlouse

Ground beetle

Harvestman

I know I'm not a snail, but can I be your friend too?

Dead log safari

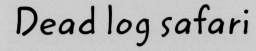

Rotting logs from dead trees are teeming with bugs! They feed on the rotting wood, and on other bugs and plants that live there.

BUG SAFETY

You may live in a place where there are biting or poisonous bugs and other animals. If you do, ask an adult to help you with this project in case something potentially dangerous is lurking under the log.

1. First, find a rotting log (this will probably be in a wood). Examine the outside of the log, and pull off pieces of rotting wood to look underneath. Use a magnifying glass to study any bugs you find.

2. Lift away dead leaves and twigs to see what's hiding under the log, but always put them back afterwards.

BUGS YOU MIGHT FIND IN A DEAD LOG

Black ant

Millipede

House spider

Snail friends

Beetle larva

Pitfall trap for bugs

Try setting up this simple trap to catch bugs that are exploring your garden during the night.

1. Take a large, clean jar to your bug-catching site (the woods or your garden). Dig a hole just big enough for the jar to fit into, so the neck of the jar is level with the ground.

2. Put a small piece of cheese in the jar to attract bugs. Place three small stones on the ground around the jar, and lay a flat rock, a piece of slate, or an old tile on top. There should be a small gap between the cover and the rim of the jar.

3. Leave the trap to do its work overnight. What bugs did you catch?

BUGS YOU MIGHT FIND IN YOUR TRAP

Centipede

Beetle

Earwig

This trap is meant for bugs! Not for rodents!

A bug hotel

Here's how to build a luxury hotel—
well, luxury for bugs!

Can birds stay
here too?

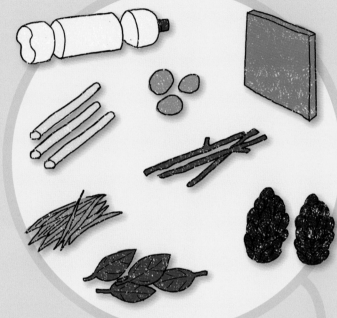

1. Find an old wooden drawer or wooden
box, about 20 x 12 inches (50 x 30 cm).

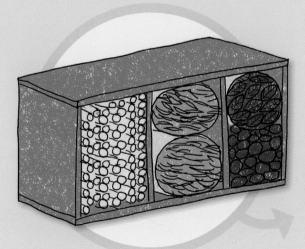

2. Insert cardboard sheets cut to size and sleeves
made of plastic bottles to divide the box into
sections. Cut short bamboo sticks, break up
twigs, and gather stones and bundles of leaves.

3. Install all your materials in the box to
complete the bug hotel.

4. Leave your bug hotel in the garden and
check every day to see what's moved in...

It's holiday
time for the
bug family!

WATCH THOSE WORMS

MAKING A WORMERY

Soil is full of earthworms! You can catch some of these fascinating creatures and make a wormery (a special home) for them. Then you can watch them at work in the soil.

Build a wormery

Ask an adult to help you with this project.

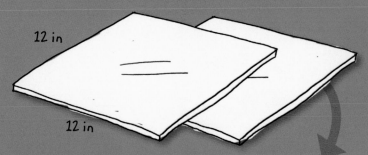

12 in

12 in

1. You need two sheets of stiff clear plastic (acrylic or Perspex), about 1 foot (30 cm) square. Find an old wooden drawer or box, about 20 x12 inches (50 x 30 cm).

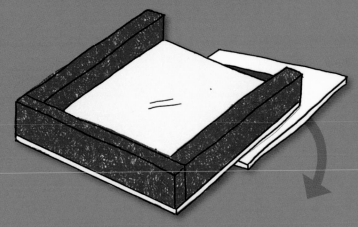

2. Next you need some strips of wood about 1 inch (3 cm) thick. Lay one of your sheets of plastic on a worktop. Then cut strips of wood to fit along three sides of the plastic, as shown. Glue the pieces on with waterproof glue.

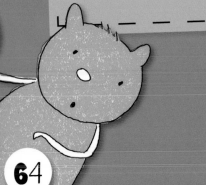

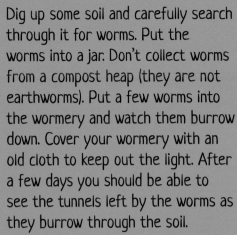

5. Dig up some soil and carefully search through it for worms. Put the worms into a jar. Don't collect worms from a compost heap (they are not earthworms). Put a few worms into the wormery and watch them burrow down. Cover your wormery with an old cloth to keep out the light. After a few days you should be able to see the tunnels left by the worms as they burrow through the soil.

3. Glue the second plastic sheet on top of the strips of wood. Wait for the glue to dry completely.

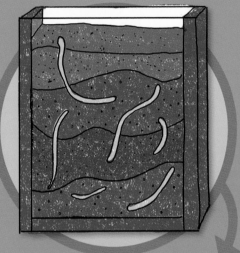

6. Gradually the worms will mix up the layers of mold, soil and sand. If the top layer is beginning to dry out, add a little more water.

4. Collect up some leaf mold, sand and soil. Put layers of mold, sand and soil into the wormery, one on top of the other. Add a little water to keep the layers damp.

7. You can also make a simple wormery in a large plastic bottle.

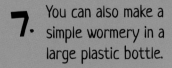
Try not to eat the worms . . .

SNAIL SAFARI

KEEPING AND RACING SNAILS

Snails are easy to find in the wild. On these pages you can find out how to collect and keep them in a snail farm, and how to hold a snail race.

Safari bat!

Start a snail farm

Ask an adult to help you with this project.

1. Find a container for your snails, such as an old, clear plastic box. Drill or puncture some holes in the lid to let in fresh air. Put plenty of food in the container for your snails: a mixture of leaves from different plants and chopped up old fruit works well.

2. Now find some snails from the wild or your garden. Search under leaves and rocks, and put the snails you find in a plastic box. At home, carefully put the snails into your snail farm. Leave the farm in a cool place out of direct sunlight to stop it from drying out.

3. Watch the snails over the next few days. Number some small stickers, then stick them carefully on the different snails to identify them.

4. Return all your snails to the wild after a few days.

Hold a snail race

Try holding a race with the snails from your farm!

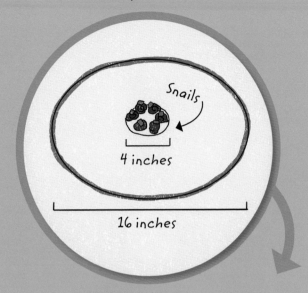

Snails

4 inches

16 inches

What's this I hear about a safari?

1. Prepare a race arena by drawing two circles on a large piece of cardstock, one about 4 inches (10 cm) across, and one about 16 inches (40 cm) across. Draw around pan lids or bowls to make the circles.

2. Mark your snails with stickers (see left) so you can identify the winner. Put all the snails in the center ring and release them. The first snail to cross the outside line wins the race!

Snail (and a beaver) on safari!

SNAIL FACTS AND FIGURES

• Snails live on land, in lakes and rivers, and in the sea.

• The giant tiger land snail grows up to 12 in. (30 cm) long.

• Snail shells are made from calcium carbonate.

• A snail has thousands of microscopic teeth.

WINGS AND WEBS

CATCHING MOTHS AND SPIDER WEBS

Dozens of different types of moths flit about during the night, when you are asleep. You can catch them quite easily to study them. The mornings are a good time to look for spider webs, which you can collect and keep.

Catching moths at night

Ask an adult to help you with this project.

1. Hang an old white sheet outdoors so that it hangs vertically, like a wall. Set up a bright light, such as a camping lamp or bright flashlight, to light up the sheet. Wait until night-time.

2. When it's dark, moths should be attracted to the light and land on the sheet. Examine them with a magnifying glass, and photograph them if you like.

Collecting spider webs

1. First, find a spider web. If a spider is in the middle of the web, blow gently and it should scuttle off. If it stays put, look for another web. Once the spider is off the web, take a handful of talcum powder in your palm and blow across it, so that the talc blows onto the web.

2. Spray a sheet of black card with hair spray. Put the card behind the web and slowly move it forward until it touches the web.

SPIDER WEB FACTS

Spider webs are incredible feats of engineering!

• The webs you are looking for in this project are called orb webs, and are made by orb-web spiders.

• Spider web silk is as strong as steel when stretched.

• Spiders use sticky and non-sticky threads to make their webs.

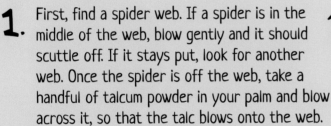

3. Pull or cut away any threads at the edges of the card, and remove the card.

4. You can make your web picture permanent with artist's fixing spray.

FOLLOW THE NEEDLE

USING A COMPASS

A compass is your most important tool for exploring in the wild. A compass needle always points to magnetic north, so you can use a compass to check which direction you are moving in. Without a compass, you might end up walking in circles!

Digital compass

Orienteering compass

Button compass with plate

Lost...

COMPASS POINTS AND DEGREES

A compass rose shows the four main directions: north, east, south, and west.

The red end of the needle always points north. An orienteering compass also shows the direction in degrees, as shown in the picture.

Following a compass

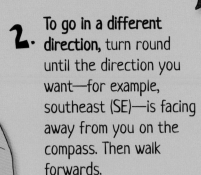

1. **Using a button compass with a plate:** hold the compass in the palm of your hand and let the plate settle. The N arrow will point north.
To walk north, turn yourself until the N is pointing directly away from you. Now you can walk forwards.

2. **To go in a different direction,** turn round until the direction you want—for example, southeast (SE)—is facing away from you on the compass. Then walk forwards.

3. **Using an orienteering compass:** turn the dial until the direction you want lines up with the red arrow on the baseplate. Hold the compass flat and turn around until the red arrow lines up with the lines on the baseplate. Then walk forwards.

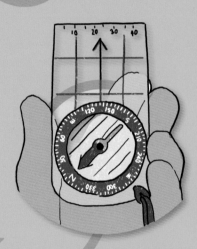

Make your own compass

If you lose your compass, you can make one with a needle and magnet.

1. Find a needle and stroke it towards the point with the north end of a bar magnet (labeled N and normally colored red). Lift the magnet away. Repeat this about twenty times. This will magnetize the needle.

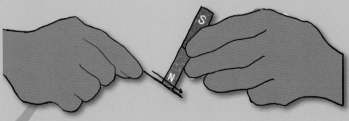

2. Place the needle on a dry leaf in a dish of water or in a puddle.

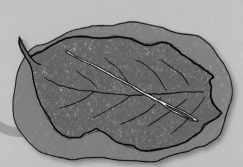

3. The leaf will slowly turn until the tip of the needle points north.

SUNSHINE SKILLS

FINDING NORTH WITHOUT A COMPASS

What if you are in the wild without a compass? You can find true north by measuring the position of the Sun and by looking for clues in the landscape.

Checking shadows

On a sunny day you can find north with just a stick!

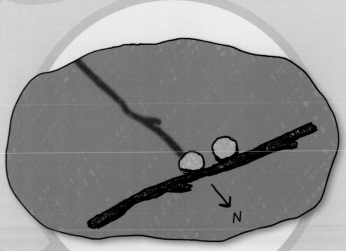

1. Find or make a stick about 47 inches (1.2 m) long, and push it a little way into the ground, making sure it's as vertical as you can get it. Mark the ground at the end of the stick's shadow with a stone.

2. Wait at least 15 minutes, then put another stone at the end of the shadow. Place another stick in line with the stones. This stick will be lined up east to west. In the northern hemisphere, north is perpendicular to it, facing away from the shadow. In the southern hemisphere, it is the other way, facing towards the shadow.

Using a watch

For this activity, you need a watch with hands, not a digital watch.

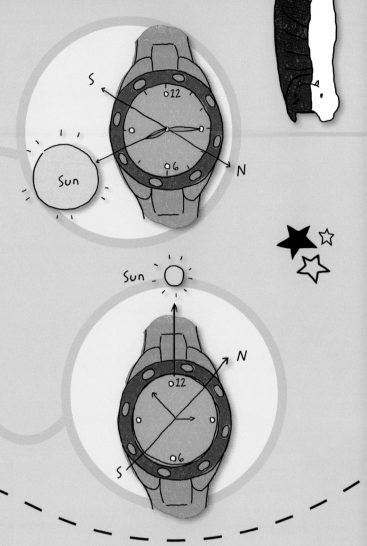

1. In the northern hemisphere, turn the watch until the hour hand points directly at the Sun. Now imagine a line halfway between the 12 on the watch face and the hour hand. That line points south, so north is the opposite way.

2. In the southern hemisphere, point the 12 on the watch face at the Sun; north is halfway between the 12 and the hour hand.

Looking at nature

If you have neither a compass nor watch, don't panic! Look for other clues to help you find north.

1. In the northern hemisphere, moss tends to grow thicker and greener on the north side of trees and walls, which are normally in shadow. In the southern hemisphere, it's the other way round.

The right-hand side of this tree faces north. →

2. In winter in the northern hemisphere, snow melts faster on the south-facing side of walls and hills, so the snowier side faces north. It's the other way round in the southern hemisphere.

Help! I'm melting!

SYMBOLS AND SCALES

READING A MAP

Maps contain lots of information about the wild places around you. They show roads and paths, rivers, hills and valleys, forests, buildings, and more. So it's good to have some map-reading skills before you go exploring.

Looking at map symbols

For this project, you need a map of your local area where you live.

—— Park boundary	▭▭ Footpath
∞ Walls	＞ Uphill path
—— Hedges and fences	▶ Access point
▭ Trees	◯ Pond
☆ View point	⌒ Picnic area
P Car park	≫ Steep uphill path
▭ Residential area / building	

1. Look for the key on your map. It shows what the symbols on the map mean.

```
0                0.5              1 mile (or 1 km)
■■■■■■■■■■■■■■■■■■■■■■■■■■■■■■■■■■■■■■■■■■■■
```
Scale = 1:25 000

2. Look for the scale on your map. This shows what a distance on the map equals in the real world. For example, on a town map, 1 inch (2 cm) on the map might be equal to 100 feet on the ground, a scale of 1 : 10,000, whereas in the above scale every 2.5 inches represents a mile.

3. Try some measuring on your map. Find two places on the map (such as your house and school, or your house and the railway station). Put the edge of a piece of paper between the two places and mark both places on the paper.

4. Now put the paper on the scale, with one mark at zero, and measure the distance.

Orientating a map

To orientate a map, you line up the map with the ground, so that things on the map match the things on the ground. You can do this by eye.

1. Stand where you can get a good view, such as on a hilltop, and then find that place on your map.

2. Search the map for landmarks, such as tall buildings, rivers, and roads, and try to find them on the landscape. Hold the map flat and turn it so that it matches the landscape.

3. All maps have north at the top, so you can orientate the map with a compass too. Hold the map flat and put your compass on top. Turn the map until the compass needle points to the top of the map.

Important note: compasses point to magnetic north, which isn't always exactly the same as "true" north on a map. Where you live there may be quite a difference between the two.

(!)

MAKE A MAP

HOW TO MAKE MAPS OF THE WILD

The brave people who explored the world hundreds of years ago had no maps. They had to make their own. Try making your own map of the place you are exploring, which might be a desert island or your local park.

He might need a bigger hill...

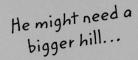

Measuring how far you walk

To make a map, you need to measure how far one landmark is from another. Do this simply by pacing: counting how many steps it takes to walk between the two places.

40 paces = 100 feet (30 m)
30 seconds = 100 feet (30 m)

1. Measure your paces first. Mark out a distance of 100 feet (30 m) along a straight path, using a tape measure or a length of string to mark every foot. Walk the 100 feet at a steady speed, counting how many double paces it takes, (count one every time your right foot hits the ground). Also time how long it takes to walk the 100 feet (30 m).

2. Multiply by two to find out how many paces or seconds it takes you to walk 200 feet (60 m). Write your answers down on a piece of paper. Now you can use these numbers to measure distance.

Make a map on the ground

Practice your mapping skills by making a map of a campsite or local park, using sticks and leaves to draw the map.

1. Clear a space on the ground for your map. Start mapping at a landmark, such as your camp, and make a simple shape to represent it.

A map made from twigs, leaves, branches and a rope

2. Now walk in a straight line to another landmark, such as a building or waterfall, counting paces as you go. Work out how far you walked, using your pacing notes.

3. Work out a scale for your map. You might use 1 inch (2 cm) on the map to equal 100 feet (30 m) in the real world. Then mark the landmark on your map, the correct distance and in the correct direction from your starting point.

Make a map from a hilltop

1. If you can find a good viewpoint, such as a hilltop, you can draw a map of the landscape around it. Mark the hilltop in the center of a piece of paper. Then estimate the distance to other landmarks. Decide a scale for your map and mark landmarks in the correct directions. Add the scale and show which way is north by using a compass.

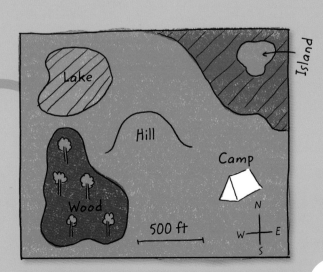

HUNT THE TREASURE!

TRY SOME GEOCACHING

Geocaching is an exploring game you can play with a GPS receiver. A GPS receiver tells you exactly where you are in the world, so you can find your position on a map. It will also guide you to landmarks. Geocaching is a good way to learn and practice GPS skills.

WHAT IS GPS?

GPS stands for Global Positioning System. A GPS receiver picks up signals from satellites and calculates its position in latitude and longitude. Some receivers are dedicated for navigation, but many mobile phones also do the job.

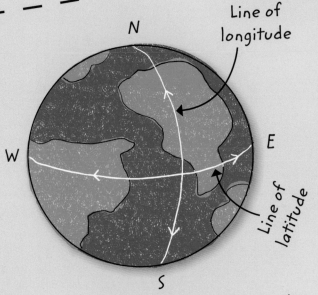

Line of longitude

Line of latitude

Your position is measured in longitude (the position north or south up and down the world) and latitude (the position east or west around the world). On a map, longitude goes up and latitude goes across.

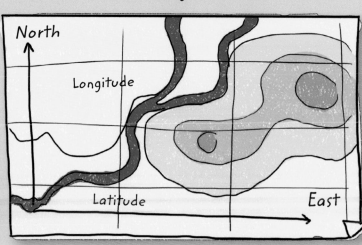

78

Leaving geocaches

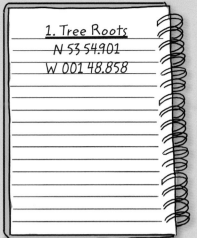

1. Tree Roots
N 53 54.901
W 001 48.858

1. Turn on your GPS unit (ask an adult to help you). Search for a good place to hide a prize, for example, between the branches of big tree. Put the prize in a plastic box to protect it. This is your first cache. Write a description of where the cache is, along with its latitude and longitude (from the GPS receiver).

1. Tree Roots
N 53 54.901
W 001 48.858

2. Fence
N 53 55.123
W 001 50.722

3. Under Rock
N 53 54.250
W 001 51.497

Adding a waypoint to a GPS receiver

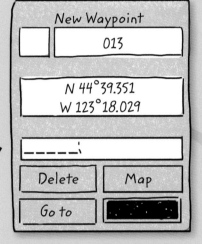

New Waypoint

013

N 44°39.351
W 123°18.029

_ _ _ _ _ '

Delete   Map

Go to

2. Find some more hiding places for some more caches. Each time, write down a clue and the latitude and longitude.

3. Give your list to your friends. They must put the latitude and longitude of your caches into their GPS receivers. They can do this by creating waypoints and giving the waypoints a name.

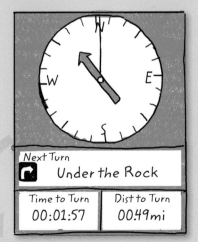

Next Turn
Under the Rock

Time to Turn
00:01:57

Dist to Turn
00.49mi

A GPS receiver showing the way to a waypoint

4. Now your friends can ask their receivers to guide them to the caches, where they can find your prizes.

5. Following the arrow on a GPS takes you to the waypoint.

6. Make sure you collect up all your prizes at the end of the day.

WILD ABOUT ROCKS

ROCKS, MINERALS, FOSSILS AND SHELLS

As you go exploring in the wild, you might climb rocks, throw rocks, skim rocks or trip over rocks! So why not add a magnifying glass to your backpack, and have a look at the rocks you find? You might be lucky and find some amazing rock and mineral samples.

Identifying different rock types

Crystals in a piece of granite, an igneous rock

ROCK TYPES

There are three types of rock:

- Igneous rocks are made when molten rock cools and becomes solid.

- Sedimentary rocks are made from layers of sand or silt.

- Metamorphic rocks are made when igneous or sedimentary rocks are changed by high temperature and immense pressure.

1. If you can see obvious crystals in a piece of rock, it is probably igneous. You might need a magnifying glass to see the crystals. Igneous rocks are also dense and heavy.

3. If the rock has a sandy, gritty feel, it is probably sedimentary. Sedimentary rocks are often quite soft and easy to break up.

Colored bands in a piece of gneiss, a metamorphic rock

Layers in a piece of sandstone, a sedimentary rock

2. If the rock has grains running through it in bands or stripes, like crystals that have been flattened, melted, and slightly mixed together, then it is probably metamorphic. These rocks are also very hard.

4. You might see layers of sedimentary rocks that are folded and twisted.

Identifying common rocks

Haha! You've been fossilized!

Basalt

Limestone

Marble

Conglomerate

Schist

Identifying common minerals

PLACES TO FIND ROCKS AND MINERALS

Hills, riverbanks, and coastlines are the best places to find exposed rocks that you can look at. Never visit steep cliffs, mines or quarries to look at rocks.

Look at a piece of igneous rock, such as granite, to see the crystals of different minerals.

The minerals in granite:
feldspar (pink)
quartz (white)
biotite (black)

Escaping from lava

Volcanoes are great places to look at rocks, but what happens if you are threatened by an erupting volcano?

1. Lava bombs come flying through the air! Try to keep an eye on them as they fall, and dodge them as you run away.

2. You can normally outrun a lava flow. Don't climb a tree or shelter in a building, as lava will simply burn them to a crisp!

Run! Lava!

VOLCANO SAFETY

Never venture near a volcano without an expert guide.

Searching for shells

You can find many different shells at the coast. They are the protective cases of sea creatures. You might find fossil shells too.

1. Collect as many different shells as you can. Compare them to these common shells.

Razor shell

Cockle shell

Whelk shell

Mussel shell

Limpet shell

Searching for fossils

Fossils are the remains of plants and animals, that lived long ago, captured in rocks. If you find a fossil, you may be looking at the bones of an animal that lived millions of years ago!

FOSSIL FORMATION

Fossils are found in sedimentary rocks. They are formed when the remains of animals and plants get trapped in layers of sediment, which turn to rock over millions of years.

1. You can find fossils where layers of some sedimentary rock are exposed, especially at the coast, and in the stones used for building, especially limestone and shale. Examine the rocks carefully. Break up the rocks into layers if you can, and look at flat faces.

Ammonite

Shark tooth

Crinoid

Brachiopod

Fern

Doh!

2. Wash any mud off your fossils in a stream, clean and dry them at home, and label them to show when and where you found them.

BIG SKIES

EXPLORING THE WEATHER

Out in the wild you are always aware of what the weather is like! Take some time to look up at the sky and you can learn a lot about how the weather works.

Should have checked the trees!

Cloud spotting

What sort of clouds can you see in the sky today? Clouds will help you to know what weather to expect.

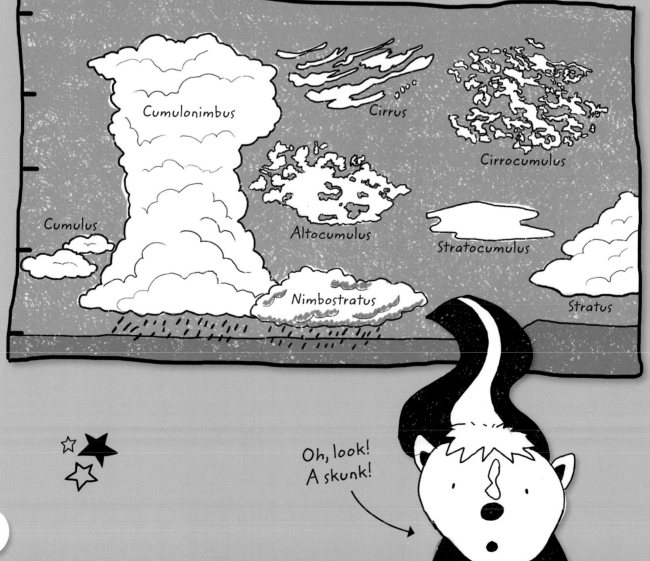

Cumulonimbus

Cirrus

Cirrocumulus

Cumulus

Altocumulus

Stratocumulus

Nimbostratus

Stratus

Oh, look! A skunk!

Predicting rain

Some clouds warn of rain on the way. Look for cirrus clouds in a clear blue sky. They show that a weather front is approaching, so you can expect rain within a few hours.

Making a rain gauge

A rain gauge measures the amount of rain that falls.

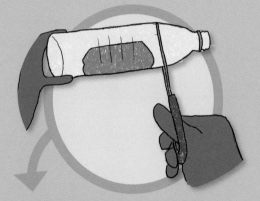

1. Cut off the top of a 2-liter plastic bottle.

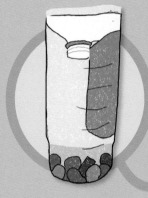

2. Put a few stones in the bottom of the bottle, to stop it from falling over, and add water to just above the curved base. Mark the water level with a pen. Put the top upside down inside the bottle.

3. Put your rain gauge in the open, where rain can fall into it. At the same time each day, measure how much the water level has risen from the previous day and record the result.

Weather clues

The prevailing wind is the direction from which the wind blows most often. Trees can show the direction of the prevailing wind.

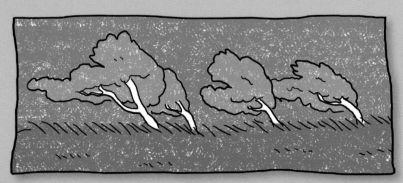

1. Look at trees on hills to see if they are bent over. The way they bend shows which way the wind normally blows. Measure the direction the wind comes from with a compass.

TAKE COVER!

AVOIDING BAD WEATHER

Some weather, such as strong winds and lightning, can be deadly. So when you are exploring the wild, it's a good idea to know how to shelter when really bad weather is on the way.

Oops.

Predicting thunder and lightning

1. Always keep an eye on the sky when exploring the wild—it could save your life! If you see clouds with anvil-shaped tops (right), a thunderstorm could be on the way.

2. Count the number of seconds between seeing lightning and hearing thunder. This tells you how far away the storm is.

Cumulonimbus clouds bring thunder and lightning.

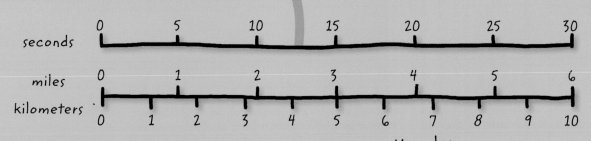

seconds	0	5	10	15	20	25	30

miles	0	1	2	3	4	5	6
kilometers	0 1	2	3 4	5	6 7	8	9 10

To measure the time between thunder and lightning, slide your finger along the top scale, then down to the bottom scale to see how far away the storm is.

Avoiding lightning in the wild

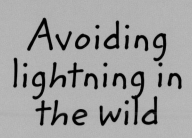

If a thunderstorm is getting closer, it's time for action...

1. If you can, go indoors or get into a vehicle. Never shelter from heavy rain under a tree, or under an umbrella, as they will attract lightning.

Safe and unsafe places to shelter during a thunderstorm

The best place to sit in the mountains

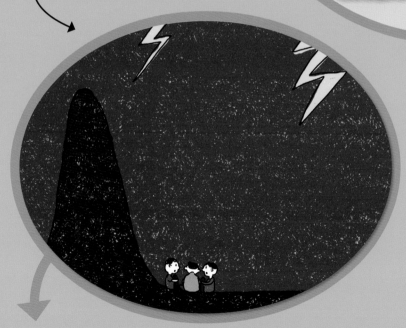

2. Lightning often strikes hilltops, so if you are on the summit of a hill, run downhill as fast as you can. Stay away from cliffs and caves, as lightning can flow down wet cliffs. Also keep away from open areas.

3. If you are caught out in the open, sit or crouch on your backpack with your feet and hands off the ground.

87

STARGAZING

NIGHT SKY WATCHING

At night in the wild, you often get a good view of the stars. That's because there are no street lights that make it hard to see them. A pair of binoculars will let you see more stars than you can with your naked eye.

Searching for constellations

Constellations are patterns made by stars in the night sky.

1. In the northern hemisphere, you should be able to find these constellations, depending on the time of year and the time of night:

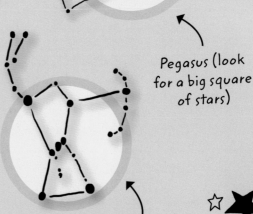

Pegasus (look for a big square of stars)

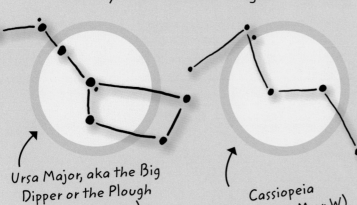

Ursa Major, aka the Big Dipper or the Plough (like a giant pan)

Cassiopeia (like a huge M or W)

Orion (shaped like an egg-timer with a belt of bright stars)

2. In the southern hemisphere, you should be able to find these constellations, depending on the time of year and the time of night:

Hydra

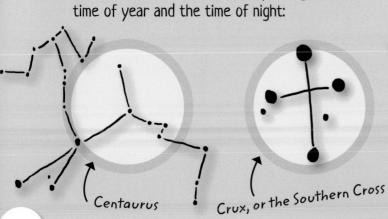

Centaurus

Crux, or the Southern Cross

3. In the southern hemisphere, you should also see two bright smudges of light. These are two galaxies called the Megallanic clouds.

Viewing the galaxy

The Milky Way is our galaxy, and is named after the bright band of light across the sky that you can see when it's very dark, as it is in the wild. The light comes from billions of stars.

Finding Polaris (the North Star) or the Southern Cross

You can navigate by the stars. Certain stars always point the way north or south.

1. In the northern hemisphere, look for the constellation of Ursa Major (right). Look along an imaginary line between the stars on the end of the pan to find a bright star. This is Polaris, the North Star or Pole.

North Star

2. In the southern hemisphere, find the Southern Cross (right). Next to the cross are two other bright stars. Imagine lines from the cross and these two stars. Where they meet is a point directly to the south.

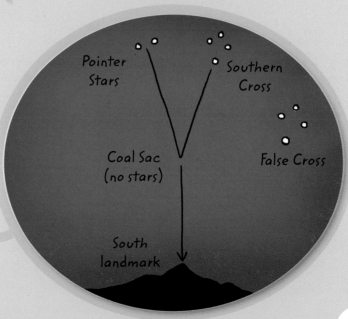

Pointer Stars

Southern Cross

Coal Sac (no stars)

False Cross

South landmark

Observing the Moon

The Moon is an amazing sight in the night sky. Some of its features are visible to the naked eye, but you can see lots of detail through a pair of binoculars. Look at the Moon on a clear night.

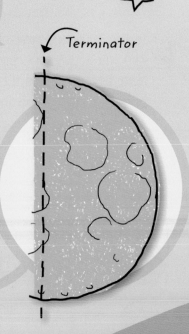

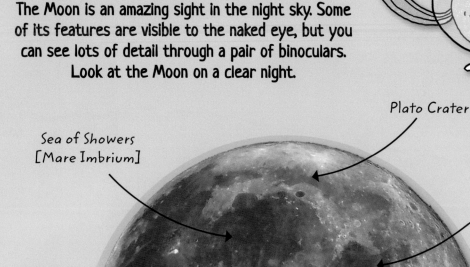

Plato Crater

Sea of Showers [Mare Imbrium]

Sea of Serenity [Mare Serenitatis]

Sea of Tranquillity [Mare Tranquillitatis]

Copernicus Crater

Sea of Crisis [Mare Crisium]

Ocean of Storms [Oceanus Procellarum]

Tycho Crater

1. The best way to look at the Moon is to sit in a chair or lie on your back, so you keep your head still. Look for light and dark areas. The dark areas are called seas, because the first astronomers thought they must be full of water. Can you identify the different seas? You might be able to see rays of dust fanning out from Tycho, a huge crater.

2. With binoculars you will be able to see dozens of craters, which you can identify with a proper Moon map. Look along the line between light and dark, called the terminator, on the Moon's surface to see detail in the craters. Put your binoculars on a tripod if you can.

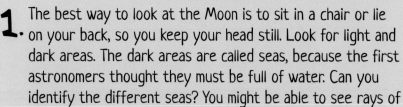

Terminator

Observing the Moon's phases

You must have seen the Moon's shape appear to change from one night to the next. Try recording these phases of the Moon.

1. Draw a series of circles on a sheet of paper. Look at the Moon at night and make a quick sketch of it inside the first circle. Repeat this each night. If you can't see the Moon, put an X through the circle.

2. After a few days, you should see that the lit area of the Moon grows until it's full, then shrinks again until you get a new Moon.

Make sure you have some food, the moon isn't really made of cheese!

NORTH BY THE MOON

You can even find north or south by looking at the Moon! When the Moon is full, use the watch system on page 73, but point the hour hand at the Moon instead of the Sun.

INDEX

You really should
be wearing a life
jacket like me!

THE AUTHOR

Chris Oxlade is an experienced author of educational books for children. He has written more than two hundred books on science, technology, sports, and hobbies, including many activity and project books. He enjoys camping and adventurous outdoor sports including rock climbing, hill running, kayaking, and sailing. He lives in England with his wife, children, and dogs.

THE ARTIST

Eva Sassin is a freelance illustrator born and bred in London. She has loved illustrating ever since she can remember, and she loves combining characters with unusual textures to give them more depth and keep them interesting.

Hmmm, which way?